THE
TAO

Lao-tzu.

THE TAO

THE SACRED WAY

edited by

TOLBERT McCARROLL

CROSSROAD · NEW YORK

1982
The Crossroad Publishing Company
575 Lexington Avenue, New York, NY 10022

Printed in the United States of America

Library of Congress Cataloging in Publication Data

Lao-tzu.
    The tao: the sacred way of Lao Tsu.

    Translation of: Tao te ching.
    I. McCarroll, Tolbert. II. Title.
BL1900.L26E5   1982   299'.51482   81-17476
ISBN 0-8245-0460-7   AACR2

Some Words of Beginning . . .

A follower of the Tao named Chuang Tzu said that wise people guide themselves with the torch of chaos and doubt. This little book cannot be understood any more than you can understand a river. If you wish to experience the river you must jump in. So it is with the *Tao Te Ching* or, as it is named here—the *Tao.*

Many things in here will confuse you. The confusion is not to be conquered. It does not result from a lack of knowledge. This confusion is a teacher that can teach you about yourself, your story, your people, your world, and the still point of the universe to which we give the crude name—the Tao.

Thomas Merton has observed that Taoist masters emphasize the gospel message, "To lose one's life is to save it, and to seek to save it for its own sake is to lose it," and "would have agreed with St. John of the Cross that you enter this kind of way when you leave all ways and, in some sense, get lost."

There are no footnotes or commentary here. These words of the Tao are to be hung like bells in our hearts and rung by the motions we make as we move through our daily lives. Any other sounds make it difficult to hear the bells.

The Tao is universal. It is not Chinese. It is found in the quest of Christian mystics, native Americans, Zen monks, desert holy men, and indeed in every culture and age in the story

·v

of the earth. Before this story began and after it ends there is the Tao. It consists of stillness and silence and it will enter into any quiet heart.

Long ago some Chinese followers of the Tao put into words the learnings of their life. Here we call these people the "Old Ones." Some probably lived more than twenty-six hundred years ago. Gradually these sayings settled together. Perhaps there was a wise one we now call "Lao Tzu" who made this collection and tied this learning together. The book is usually referred to as the *Tao* (path or way) *Te* (virtue) *Ching* (sacred book).

There are many translations of this book; all are different and all are the same. None are accurate and none are false. Ancient Chinese writing was not limited by the desire for preciseness. It more resembled a series of pictures. The people who would learn the message must swim in the characters and in the spaces around them. What is not written is equal in importance to what is written. Nothing can be seen by examining a page of the book, unless at the same moment you examine your own heart.

There are three terms that appear often.

The Tao (pronounced something like "Dau"). Half of the character starts with some hair joined to a head. That made "head." The other half has three parts in it: to step with the left foot and to halt and to walk step by step. From these comes a feeling of wholeness; head and foot, round and square, stop and go. Tao is not a phenomenon or a being. Some medieval Christian mystics distinguished between "God" and the "Godhead." Perhaps the Tao and the Godhead are the same concepts. By its very nature the Tao is unfathomable, yet it can be relied upon. Once you have given up your ideas of what the Tao is, turn to chapter 25 and read a description of it.

Te (pronounced something like "Tuh"). This means "Virtue" or the moral force and strength that comes from living a consistent and whole life. The character is made of three parts: "to go"/ "straight"/"to the heart." It is not a prissy virtue, but like the Latin word *vir* from which "virtue" stems, Te reflects a strength. Te is the manifestation of the Tao that is produced through the instrument of people, animals, plants, and all things that are completely committed to being themselves. There is nothing mysterious about acquiring Virtue. If you eat well you are not undernourished. If you exercise you get strong. If you follow the Tao you obtain Virtue.

Shung Ren. This is usually translated the "Sage" or "Wise Man." Looking at the history of the phrase, I feel it means "a person who has a duty to listen." I have searched for a lot of words to express this and for a while used the word "Saint." In Western languages it meant a holy person. The word "holy" intertwined in Old English with concepts of wholeness and health. But there are too many connotations to "Saint," so I settled on a parallel concept used by the ancient followers of the Tao and usually translated "True Person." This book is written for those who wish to heed the call to completeness by becoming more courageously themselves, learning to be more at home on the earth and living in such a way as to add some pure and still moments to the rhythm of life in which all share.

I divided this work into two books. This follows an ancient practice. The first book was sometimes called "Classic of Tao" and the second was given the name "Classic of Te." There is a difference and a sameness about the two books—like breathing in and breathing out.

The way of Tao does not lead anywhere; the road itself is the journey. There are a lot of interesting things in this book and you can wander down many side paths. But the main road is called "oneness."

When we look out or in we usually see parts or conflicts. At such times assume that what appears as two is not two. Then what do you see?

Sony Ts'an has written:

To trust in the heart is the "not two"
The "not two" is to trust in the heart.

Trust leads to a surrender to the now-moment, no worry about making the future or remaking the past. Little by little we learn to live a less self-centered life. Through the lessons of everyday living we learn to become free of our desires. Gradually we begin the journey home, to the place where we do not have to prove ourselves or anything else.

The men and women at Starcross Monastery are Christian monks and nuns who have found this book of great value in that pilgrimage which leads home to God. This is not just a book in our library but one that has rested in our chapel, on our work benches, by our beds, in our backpacks and pockets. Each day we read a chapter and try to live with it. As we have done this over the years we have come to realize that we hold a flower that will never stop unfolding. May this flower now grow well in your garden.

Tolbert McCarroll

Starcross Monastery, Annapolis, California

Here Begin
The Sayings of
The Old Ones

THE
FIRST
BOOK

·**1**·

The Tao that can be spoken of is not the eternal Tao.
The name that can be named is not the eternal name.

The nameless is the beginning of heaven and earth.
The named is the mother of the ten thousand things.

Send your desires away and you will see the mystery.
Be filled with desire
    and you will see only the manifestation.

As these two come forth they differ in name.
Yet at their source they are the same.
This source is called a mystery.

Darkness within darkness,
    the gateway to all mystery.

All under heaven see beauty as beauty
        only because they also see ugliness.
All announce that good is good
        only because they also denounce what is bad.

Therefore, something and nothing give birth to one another.
Difficult and easy complete one another.
Long and short fashion one another.
High and low arise from one another.
Notes and tones harmonize with one another.
Front and back follow one another.

Thus, the True Person acts without striving
        and teaches without words.

Deny nothing to the ten thousand things.
Nourish them without claiming authority,
Benefit them without demanding gratitude,
Do the work, then move on.

And, the fruits of your labor will last forever.

·3·

Not exalting the talented prevents rivalry.
Not valuing goods that are hard to obtain
    prevents stealing.
Not displaying desirable things
    prevents confusion of the heart.

Therefore, the True Person governs by
    emptying the heart of desire
    and filling the belly with food,
    weakening ambitions
    and strengthening bones.
If the people are simple and free from desire,
    then the clever ones never dare to interfere.

Practice action without striving
    and all will be in order.

·4·

The Tao is like an empty bowl,
    yet it may be used
    without ever needing to be filled.
It is the deep and unfathomable source
    of the ten thousand things.

Blunt the sharpness.
Untie the knot.
Soften the glare.
Settle with the dust.

It is hidden deep yet ever present.
I do not know whose child it is.
It existed before the common ancestor.

·5·

Heaven and earth are not moved
    by offerings of straw-dogs.
The True Person is not moved
    by offerings of straw-dogs.

The space between heaven and earth is like a bellows.
It is empty and yet never exhausted.
The more it works the more comes out.

Many words lead to exhaustion.
Better to hold fast to your center.

·6·

The valley spirit never dies.
It is the unknown first mother,
    whose gate is the root
    from which grew heaven and earth.
It is dimly seen, yet always present.
Draw from it all you wish;
    it will never run dry.

·7·

Heaven and earth last forever.
The reason why heaven and earth last forever
    is that they do not live for themselves.
Hence, they last forever.

Therefore, the True Person
    leaves self behind
    and thus is found in front,
    is not guarded and thus is preserved,
    is self-free and thus is able
    to find fulfillment.

·**8**·

The highest good is like water.
For water benefits the ten thousand things without striving.
It settles in places that people avoid
    and so is like the Tao. ⟋

In choosing your home look to the land.
In preparing your heart go deep.
In associating with others value gentleness.
In speaking exhibit good faith.
In governing provide good order.
In the conduct of business be competent.
In action be timely.

When there is no strife, nothing goes amiss.

·9·

Better to stop in time than to fill to the brim.
Hone a blade to the sharpest point,
    and it will soon be blunt.
Fill your house with gold and jade,
    and no one can protect it.
Be prideful about wealth and position,
    and you bring disasters upon yourself.
Retire when the work is done.
This is the way of heaven.

·10·

While carrying your active life on your head
　　can you embrace the quiet spirit in your arms,
　　and not let go?
While being fully focused on your vital breath
　　can you make it soft like that of a newborn babe?
While cleaning your inner mirror
　　can you leave it without blemish?
While loving the people and ruling the country
　　can you dispense with cleverness?
While opening and closing the gates of heaven
　　can you be like a mother bird?
While penetrating the four quarters with your insight
　　can you remain simple?

Help the people live!
Nourish the people!

Help them live yet lay no claim to them.
Benefit them yet seek no gratitude.
Guide them yet do not control them.
This is called the hidden Virtue.

·11·

Thirty spokes connect to the wheel's hub;
>   yet, it is the center hole
>   that makes it useful.
Clay is shaped into a vessel;
>   yet, it is the emptiness within
>   that makes it useful.
Doors and windows are cut for a room;
>   yet it is the space where there is nothing
>   that makes it useful.

Therefore, though advantage comes from what is;
>   usefulness comes from what is not.

·12·

The five colors blind the eye.
The five notes deafen the ear.
The five flavors dull the palate.
Racing and hunting drive the heart wild.
Goods that are hard to obtain hinder the journey.

Therefore, the True Person
    is guided more by the belly than the eye,
    and prefers this within to that without.

·13·

Both favor and disgrace bring fear.
Great trouble comes from having a body.

What is meant by:
    "Both favor and disgrace bring fear"?
Favor leads to a fear of losing it and
    disgrace leads to a fear of greater trouble.

What is meant by:
    "Great trouble comes from having a body"?
The reason you have trouble is that
    you are self-conscious.
No trouble can befall a self-free person.

Therefore, surrender your self-interest.
Love others as much as you love yourself.
Then you can be entrusted with all things under heaven.

·14·

Look at it, you cannot see it.
It is invisible.
Listen to it, you cannot hear it.
It is inaudible.
Reach for it, you cannot grasp it.
It is intangible.

These three qualities are unfathomable
    and so they fuse together and become one.

The upper part is not bright.
The lower part is not dark.
Ceaselessly the Unnamed moves back to nothingness.
It has the form of the formless,
    the image of the imageless.
It is indefinable and shadowy.
Go up to it and you will not see its front.
Follow it and you will not see its back.

Yet, hold fast to this ancient Tao and
    you will experience the present now-moment.

Know its beginnings and
    you can follow the path of the Tao.

·15·

The ancient followers of the Tao
      were subtle, mysterious, and penetrating.
They were too deep to be fathomed.
All we can do is describe their appearance.
Hesitant, as if crossing a winter stream.
Watchful, as if aware of neighbors on all sides.
Respectful, like a visiting guest.
Yielding, like ice beginning to melt.
Simple, like an uncarved block.
Open, like a valley.
Obscure, like muddy water.

Who else can be still and let the muddy water
      slowly become clear?
Who else can remain at rest and slowly come to life?

Those who hold fast to the Tao
      do not try to fill themselves to the brim.
Because they do not try to be full
      they can be worn out and yet ever new.

·16·

Empty everything out;
     hold fast to your stillness.
Even though all things are stirring together,
     watch for the movement of return.
The ten thousand things flourish and then
     each returns to the root from which it came.
Returning to the root is stillness.
Through stillness each fulfills its destiny.
That which has fulfilled its destiny
     becomes part of the Always-so.
To be aware of the Always-so is to awaken.

Those who innovate while in ignorance of the Always-so
     move toward disaster.
Those who act with awareness of the Always-so
     embrace all, are not possessed by particular desire.
     and move toward the Tao.
Those who are at one with the Tao abide forever.
Even after their bodies waste away,
     they are safe and whole.

·17·

The best leader is one whose existence
    is barely known by the people.
Next comes one whom they love and praise.
Next comes one they fear.
Next comes one they defy.

If you do not trust enough, you will not be trusted.

True Persons do not offer words lightly.
When their task is accomplished
    and their work is completed,
        the people say, "It happened to us naturally."

·18·

When the great Tao is forgotten,
  benevolence and moral codes arise.
When shrewdness and cleverness appear,
  great hypocrisy follows.
When there is no harmony in the family,
  filial manners are developed.
When the country is in disorder,
  ministers appear as loyal servants.

·19·

Stop being learned and your troubles will end.

Give up wisdom, discard cleverness,
and the people will benefit a hundredfold.

Give up benevolence, discard moral judgments,
and the people will rediscover natural compassion.

Give up shrewdness, discard gain,
and thieves and robbers will disappear.

These three false adornments are not enough to live by.
They must give way to something more solid.
Look for what is simple and hold onto the Uncarved Block.
Diminish thoughts of self and restrain desires.

·20·

How great is the difference between "yea" and "yeah"?
How great is the distinction between "good" and "evil"?

Must I fear what others fear? How silly!

Everyone else is joyous as if enjoying the greatest feast,
    or going up the terraces in spring.
I alone am drifting without direction,
    like a baby who has not yet smiled.
I alone am moping as if I had no home.
Everyone else has more than they need,
    I alone seem in want.
I have the mind of a fool, how confused I am!
Other people are bright and clever,
    I alone am dark.
Other people are alert and self-assured,
    I alone am dull and muddled.
I am unsettled like the waves of the sea,
    like the restless wind.
Everyone else has a purpose,
    I alone am stubborn and awkward.
I am different from other people,
Even so, I am nourished by the Great

·21·

The Great Virtue is to follow the Tao and only the Tao.

The Tao is shadowy and intangible.
Intangible and evasive, and yet within it is a form.
Evasive and intangible, and yet within it is a substance.
Shadowy and dark, and yet within it is a vital force.
This vital force is real and can be relied upon.

From ancient times to the present the Tao's instructions
    have not been forgotten.
Through it can be perceived the beginning of the story
    of life.
How do I know how it was at the beginning of the story
    of life?
Because of what is within me.

·22·

Yield and overcome;
        bend and be straight.
Empty out and be full;
        wear out and be renewed.
Have little and gain;
        have much and be confused.

Therefore, the True Person embraces the One
        and becomes a model for all.

Do not look only at yourself,
        and you will see much.
Do not justify yourself,
        and you will be distinguished.
Do not brag,
        and you will have merit.
Do not be prideful,
        and your work will endure.

It is because you do not strive
        that no one under heaven can strive with you.

The saying of the Old Ones, "Yield and Overcome,"
        is not an empty phrase.
True wholeness is achieved
        by blending with life.

·23·

To talk little is to follow nature.

A whirlwind does not last all morning.
A sudden shower does not last all day.
Who produces these things?
Heaven and earth!
Even heaven and earth cannot make
    wild things last long.
How then can people hope to do so?

People of the Tao
    conform to the Tao.
People of Virtue
    conform to Virtue.
People who lose the way
    conform to the loss.
Those who conform to the Tao
    are welcomed into the Tao.
Those who conform to Virtue
    are welcomed into Virtue.
Those who conform to the loss
    are welcomed into the loss.

Those who do not trust enough
    will not be trusted.

·24·

The person on tiptoe is not steady.
The person with legs astride cannot walk.

Those who look only at themselves see little.
Those who justify themselves are not distinguished.
Those who brag have no merit.
The work of prideful people will not endure.

From the standpoint of the Tao,
    these things are
    "excessive food and tumors of the body."
As they bring sickness,
    followers of the Tao do not linger around them.

·25·

Something formless yet complete,
     existing before heaven and earth.
Silent and limitless,
     it stands alone and does not change.
Reaching everywhere, it does not tire.
Perhaps it is the Mother of all things under heaven.
I do not know its name
     so I call it "Tao."

When I have to describe it I call it "great."
Being great it flows.
It flows far away.
Having gone far away, it returns.

Therefore, the Tao is great.
Heaven is great.
Earth is great.
People are also great.
Thus, people constitute one of the
four great things of the universe.

People conform to the earth.
The earth conforms to heaven.
Heaven conforms to the Tao.
The Tao conforms to its own nature.

·26·

The solid must be the root of the light.
The still must be the master of the restless.

Therefore, wise people when traveling all day
    do not lose sight of their baggage cart.
Although there are beautiful scenes to see,
    they remain quietly in their own place.
Should a lord of ten thousand chariots
    appear more frivolous than a simple traveler?

To be light is to lose the root.
To be restless is to lose the master.

·27·

A skillful traveler leaves no track.
A skillful speaker makes no slip.
A skillful reckoner needs no counting rod.
A skillfully made door requires no bolts,
    yet it cannot be opened.
A skillful binding has no cords or knots,
    yet it cannot be untied.

Therefore, the True Person is skillful in assisting people,
    and abandons nobody;
Is skillful in assisting things,
    and abandons nothing.
This is called "Following the Inner Light."

Therefore, the skillful person is the teacher
    of the person without skill.
The person without skill is the material
    for the skillful person.
If you do not respect the teacher,
    if you do not care for the material,
    you are on the road to confusion
    and your cleverness will not save you.

This is an essential principle.

·28·

Develop the strength of a man,
   but live as gently as a woman.
Become a brook and receive all things under heaven.
If you are such a brook
   then Virtue will constantly flow into you
   and you will become a simple child again.

Know the pure
   but live the life of the sullied.
Become a fountain to all things under heaven.
If you become such a fountain
   then you will have abundant Virtue
   and you will return to the state of the Uncarved Block.

When the Uncarved Block is cut up into pieces,
   it is turned into specialized instruments.
But the True Person makes use of it whole
   and becomes the master of the instruments.

Hence, it is said, "The finest carver cuts little."

·29·

Whoever wishes to take over the world
    will not succeed.
The world is a sacred vessel
    and nothing should be done to it.
Whoever tries to tamper with it
    will mar it.
Whoever tries to grab it
    will lose it.

Hence, there is a time to go ahead
    and a time to stay behind.
There is a time to breathe easy
    and a time to breathe hard.
There is a time to be vigorous
    and a time to be gentle.
There is a time to gather
    and a time to release.

Therefore, the True Person avoids extremes,
    self-indulgence, and extravagance.

·30·

If you would assist leaders of people
      by way of the Tao,
you will oppose the use of armed force to overpower
      the world.

Those who use weapons will be harmed by them.
Where troops have camped only thorn bushes grow.
Bad harvests follow in the wake of a great army.

The skillful person strikes the blow and stops,
      without taking advantage of victory.
Bring it to a conclusion but do not be vain.
Bring it to a conclusion but do not be boastful.
Bring it to a conclusion but do not be arrogant.
Bring it to a conclusion but only when there is no choice.
Bring it to a conclusion but without violence.

When force is used, youthful strength decays.
This is not the way of Tao.
And that which goes against the Tao
      will quickly pass away.

·**31**·

Weapons are ill-omened things.

Among gentle people the left side
  is the place of honor when at home,
  but in war the right side is the place of honor.

Weapons are not proper instruments for gentle people;
  they use them only when they have no other choice.
Peace and quiet are what they value.
They do not glory in victory.
To glorify it is to delight in the slaughter of people.
Those who delight in the slaughter of people will
  never thrive among all that dwell under heaven.

The army that has killed people
  should be received with sorrow.
Conquerors should be received with the rites of mourning.

·32·

The Tao is forever nameless.

Though the Uncarved Block is small,
    it is not inferior to anything under heaven.
If leaders could keep hold of it,
    the ten thousand things would submit to them freely.
Heaven and earth would unite and sweet dew would fall.
The people would live in harmony
    without any law or decree.

Only when the Block is carved are there names.
As soon as there are names
    it is time to stop.
Knowing when to stop prevents trouble.

All under heaven will return to the Tao
    as brooks and streams flow home to the sea.

·33·

Knowing others is to be clever.
Knowing yourself is to be enlightened.
Overcoming others requires force.
Overcoming yourself requires strength.

To know that you have enough is to be rich.
Push through and you may get your way,
    but return home and you will endure.
Live out your days and you have had a long life.

·34·

The great Tao covers everything like a flood.
It flows to the left and to the right.
The ten thousand things depend upon it
    and it denies none of them.
It accomplishes its task yet claims no reward.
It clothes and feeds the ten thousand things
    yet it does not attempt to control them.
Therefore, it may be called "the little."

The ten thousand things return to it,
    even though it does not control them.
Therefore, it may be called "the great."

So it is that the True Person does not wish to be great
    and therefore becomes truly great.

·35·

Hold on to the Great Image
    and all under heaven will approach you.
Coming to you and not being harmed,
    they will find rest, peace, and security.

A passing guest will pause at the sound of music
    and the smell of fancy food.
By comparison the Tao is mild and flavorless.
It is not solid enough to be seen,
    nor loud enough to be heard.
Yet, it lasts forever.

·36·

That which is to be shrunk
  must first be stretched out.
That which is to be weakened
  must first be strengthened.
That which is to be cast down
  must first be raised up.
That which is to be taken
  must first be given.

There is wisdom in dimming your light.
For the soft and gentle
  will overcome the hard and powerful.

Fish are best left in deep waters.
And, weapons are best kept out of sight.

·37·

The Tao never strives,
     yet nothing is left undone.
If leaders were able to adhere to it
     the ten thousand things would develop
     of their own accord.
If after they have developed
     they experience desires to strive,
     they can bury those desires
     under the nameless Uncarved Block.

The nameless Uncarved Block can protect
     against desire.
When desires are restrained there will be peace,
     and then all under heaven will be at rest.

THE
SECOND
BOOK

·38·

A person of high virtue is not conscious of virtue
    and therefore possesses Virtue.
A person of little virtue tries to be virtuous
    and therefore lacks Virtue.
A person of high virtue does not make a fuss
    and is not seen.
A person of little virtue always makes a fuss
    and is always seen.
A truly good person functions without ulterior motive.
A moralist acts out of private desires.
A ritualist acts and, when no one responds,
    rolls up a sleeve and marches.

When we lose the Tao, we turn to Virtue.
When we lose Virtue, we turn to kindness.
When we lose kindness, we turn to morality.
When we lose morality, we turn to ritual.

Ritual is the mere husk of good faith and loyalty
    and the beginning of disorder.
Knowledge of what is to come
    may be a flower of the Tao,
    but it is the beginning of folly.

Hence, the well-formed person relies on what is solid
    and not on what is flimsy,
    on the fruit and not the flower.
Therefore, such a person lets go of that without
    and is content with this within.

·39·

From ancient times these things have arisen from the One:

Heaven is clear because of the One,
The earth is firm because of the One,
The Spirit is strong because of the One,
The valley is full because of the One,
The ten thousand things reproduce because of the One,
Leaders are able to lead because of the One.

All of this comes from the One.

If heaven were not clear it would soon split.
If the earth were not firm it would soon bend and break.
If the Spirit were not strong it would soon wear out.
If the valley were not full it would soon dry up.
If the ten thousand things did not reproduce
    they would soon die out.
If leaders could not lead they would soon fall.

Therefore, greatness has its source in the little.
The low is the foundation of the high.

Princes call themselves "alone," "helpless," "worthless."
Is this not acknowledging a humble root?

Enumerate the parts of a carriage
    and you have not defined a carriage.

Better to resound like stone chimes
    than to tinkle like jade bells.

·40·

Returning is the direction of the Tao.
Yielding is the way of the Tao.

The ten thousand things are born of Being
    and Being is born of Nonbeing.

·41·

The wise student on hearing the Tao
    diligently puts it into practice.
The average student on hearing the Tao
    keeps it one minute and loses it the next.
The mediocre student on hearing the Tao
    laughs at it loudly.
If this student did not laugh it would not be the Tao.

Therefore, the ancient proverb says:

    The bright path seems dull.
    The path that goes forward seems to lead backward.
    The even path seems up and down.
    The greatest whiteness seems soiled.

    High Virtue seems like a canyon.
    Abundant Virtue seems deficient.
    Vigorous Virtue seems limp.
    Simple Virtue seems faded.

    The greatest square has no corners.
    The greatest vessel takes long to complete.
    The greatest note is hard to hear.
    The greatest image has no shape.

The Tao is hidden and nameless;
    yet, it is the Tao alone that supports all things
    and brings them to completion.

·42·

The Tao gives birth to the One.
The One gives birth to two.
Two gives birth to three.
And three gives birth to the ten thousand things.

The ten thousand things have their backs in the shadow
    while they embrace the light.
Harmony is achieved by blending
    the breaths of these two forces.

People dislike the words "alone," "helpless," "worthless,"
    yet this is how Princes describe themselves.

So it is that sometimes a thing is increased
    by being diminished and
    diminished by being increased.

What others teach I also teach:
    "A violent person will not die a natural death."
I shall make this the basis of my teaching.

·**43**·

The most yielding of all things
    overcomes the hardest of all things.
That which has no substance
    enters where there is no crevice.

Hence, I know the value of action without striving.

Few things under heaven bring more benefit than
    the lessons learned from silence and
    the actions taken without striving.

·44·

Your integrity or your body:
    Which is more important?
Your body or your possessions:
    Which is worth more?
Gain or loss:
    Which is more harmful?
Thus it is that the miser will pay much.
The hoarder will suffer great loss.
Be content with what you have
    and you will not be disgraced.
Know when to stop
    and you will be preserved from danger.
Only in this way will you long endure.

·45·

Great accomplishment seems incomplete,
      yet its use is not impaired.
Great fullness seems empty,
      yet it will never be drained.

Great straightness looks crooked.
Great skill appears clumsy.
Great eloquence sounds like stammering.

Movement overcomes cold,
      stillness overcomes heat.

The calm and quiet set right
      everything under heaven.

·46·

When the Tao prevails in the world
    swift horses are used to fertilize the fields.
When the Tao is unheeded
    war horses are bred on the border lands.

There is no greater offense than harboring desires.
There is no greater disaster than discontent.
There is no greater misfortune than wanting more.

Hence, if you are content
You will always have enough.

·47·

Without going outside
    you can know the ways of the world.
Without looking through the window
    you can see the way of heaven.
The farther you go
    the less you know.

Therefore, the True Person
    arrives without traveling,
    perceives without looking,
    and acts without striving.

·**48**·

In the pursuit of learning,
    every day something is added.
In the pursuit of the Tao,
    every day something is dropped.

Less and less is done
    until you come to action with striving.
When you follow this practice,
    nothing remains undone.

All under heaven is won by
    letting things take their course.
Nothing can be gained by interfering.

·**49**·

The True Person does not have an individual heart
    but uses the heart of the people.

I am kind to those who are kind.
I am also kind to those who are not kind.
Thus, there is an increase in kindness.
I keep faith with those who are in good faith.
I also keep faith with those who lack good faith.
Thus, there is an increase of good faith.

The True Person is detached and humble
    and to the world appears confusing.
The people all strain their eyes and ears,
    yet the True Person remains childlike.

·50·

When going off one way means living
    and going off the other way means dying,
    three in ten are companions of Life,
    three in ten are companions of Death, and
    three in ten value Life but drift toward Death.

Why is all this so?
Because, these people are too greedy about living.

It is said:
    People who are skillful in caring
    for the life that has been given to them
    travel abroad without fear of wild ox or tiger,
    and enter a battle without concern for sharp weapons.
    There is no place for the wild ox to thrust its horns,
    there is no place for the tiger to put its claws,
    there is no place for a weapon to lodge.

How is this so?
Because, there is no place for Death to enter in!

·**51**·

The Tao gives life to all things,
    and its Virtue nourishes them,
    forms each according to its nature
    and gives to each its inner strength.

Therefore, the ten thousand things all venerate the Tao
    and honor its Virtue.
It has never been decreed that the Tao be venerated
    and its Virtue be honored;
    they have always been so treated spontaneously.

Thus, the Tao gives life to all things;
    and its Virtue raises them, nourishes them,
    brings them to their full growth,
    feeds, shelters, and protects them.

Giving life without claiming authority,
    benefiting without demanding gratitude,
    guiding without control.
This is called hidden Virtue.

·52·

All things under heaven had a common beginning,
　　and that beginning could be considered
　　the Mother of all things.
When you know the Mother
　　you will also know the children.
Know the children, yet hold fast to the Mother,
　　and to the end of your days
　　you will be free from danger.

Block the passages!
Shut the doors!
And, to the end of your days
　　your strength will not fail you.
Open the passages!
Increase your activities!
And, to the end of your days
　　you will be beyond help.

See the small and develop clear vision.
Practice yielding and develop strength.
Use the outer light to return to the inner light,
　　and save yourself from harm.

This is known as following the Always-so.

·**53**·

If I have even a little sense,
    I will walk upon the great path of Tao
    and only fear straying from it.
This Great Way is straight and smooth
    yet people often prefer the side roads.

The courtyard is well kept
    but the fields are full of weeds,
    and the granaries stand empty.
Still, there are those of us
    who wear elegant clothes, carry sharp swords,
    pamper ourselves with food and drink
    and have more possessions than we can use.
These are the actions of robbers.

This is certainly far from the Tao.

·54·

What is well rooted cannot be pulled up.
What is firmly grasped will not slip loose.
It will be honored from generation to generation.

When cultivated in your person, Virtue will be real.
When cultivated in your household, Virtue will be plentiful.
When cultivated in your village, Virtue will endure.
When cultivated in your country, Virtue will abound.
When cultivated in your world, Virtue will be universal.

Hence, through yourself look at Self.
Through your household look at Household.
Through your community look at Community.
Through your country look at Country.
Through your world look at World.

How do I know that the world is like this?
Because of what is within me.

·55·

A person who is filled with Virtue
　　is like a newborn child.
Poisonous insects will not sting,
　　wild animals will not pounce,
　　birds of prey will not swoop down.
Although bones are soft and sinews weak,
　　a child's grip is firm.
The union of man and woman is not known,
　　yet there is completeness,
　　because a child's vital force is at its height.
Crying all day will not produce hoarseness,
　　because there is perfect harmony.

To know harmony is to know the Always-so.
To know the Always-so is to be awakened.

Trying to fill life to the brim invites a curse.
For the mind to make demands upon the breath of life
　　brings strain.

Whatever has been forced to a peak of vigor
　　approaches its decay.
This is not the way of Tao.
And that which goes against the Tao
　　will quickly pass away.

·**56**·

Those who know do not speak.
Those who speak do not know.

Block the passages!
Shut the doors!
Blunt the sharpness!
Untangle the knots!
Soften the glare!
Settle with the dust!
This is the Mystery of Evenness.

Those who have achieved this cannot be enclosed
        nor kept at a distance;
        they cannot be benefited nor harmed,
        honored nor disgraced.

Therefore, this is the noblest state under heaven.

·57·

Govern the country by being straightforward.
Wage war by being crafty.
Win all under heaven by not meddling.

How do I know that this is so?
By what is within me.

The more restrictions there are,
     the poorer are the people.
The more pointed the people's weapons,
     the more disorder there is in the country.
The more ingenious and clever the people,
     the more strange the contrivances that appear.
The more laws and edicts that are posted,
     the more thieves and robbers that arise.

Hence an Old One has said:
     I act without striving and the
          people transform themselvey.
     I love stillness and the
          people straighten themselves.
     I do not meddle and the
          people prosper by themselves.
     I am free from desires and the
          people themselves return to the simplicity
          of the Uncarved Block.

·58·

When the government is unseen
    the people are simple and happy.
When the government is lively
    the people are cunning and discontented.

On misery perches happiness.
Beneath happiness crouches misery.

Who knows when this will cease?
The straight changes into the crooked.
The good becomes the ominous.
Surely the people
    have been confused for a long time.

Therefore, the True Person squares without cutting,
    carves without hacking,
    straightens without dislocating,
    gives forth light without blinding.

·59·

For governing others and serving heaven
    there is nothing better than moderation.
A person who is moderate returns to the path.
Returning to the path brings an abundance of Virtue.
This good store of Virtue cannot be conquered.
Virtue that cannot be conquered knows no limit.
Only a person who has limitless Virtue is fit to lead.
Only the leader who possesses the Mother of the country
    will long endure.
This is called making the roots go deep
    by restraining the trunk.
Learn to focus your life and you will see many days.

·60·

Governing a big country is like cooking a small fish.

Let all under heaven be governed in accordance with the Tao,
    and demons will not manifest their power.
It is not that they lack power
    but rather they will not use their power
    to harm the people.
They are not the only ones who have power
    and do not use it to harm the people.
The True Person does not harm the people.
Whenever there is no harm done,
    that power flows into the common Virtue.

·61·

A great country is like the low lands
    where all the streams unite.

In all things under heaven
    the female overcomes the male by her stillness,
    and because she is still she lies below.

Hence, if the great country will take the low place
    it will win over the little country.
If the little country will take the low place
    it will win over the great country.

Thus, the one gets below and prospers
    and the other remains below and prospers.
All that the great country wants is more people.
All that the little country wants is a place
    for its people to go and to be employed.
If each is to get what it wants
    it is necessary for the great country
    to take the low place.

·62·

The Tao is to the ten thousand things
    what the shrine is in the home.
It is the treasure of the virtuous
    and the protection of the wrongdoer.

Good words are appreciated.
Good deeds are accepted as gifts.

Even the wrongdoers are not abandoned.

Hence, on the day an Emperor is installed
    and appoints the three ducal ministers,
    remain where you are and make an offering of the Tao.
It will be preferable to a gift of jade discs
    followed by a team of four horses.
Why did the ancients value the Tao?
Was it not because through it
    you can find what you seek,
    and because of it
    you can escape what is hounding you?

Therefore, it is the most valuable thing under heaven.

·63·

Act without striving.
Work without interfering.
Find the flavor in what is flavorless.

Enlarge the small, increase the few.
Heal injury with goodness.

Handle the difficult while it is still easy.
Cultivate the great while it is still small.

All difficult things begin as easy things.
All great things begin as small things.

Therefore, the True Person never attempts anything great,
    and accomplishes great things.

Lightly made promises inspire little faith.
Trying to make things easy results in great difficulties.

Therefore, the True Person regards everything as difficult,
    and is never overcome by difficulties.

·64·

Peace is easily maintained while things are still at rest.
Trouble is easily handled before it starts.
What is brittle is easily broken.
What is minute is easily scattered.

Handle a problem before it appears.
Secure order before confusion begins.

A tree as big as a person's embrace begins as a tiny shoot.
A terrace nine stories high rises from a shovelful of earth.
A journey of a thousand miles begins under your feet.

A person who interferes does harm,
    and those who grasp lose their hold.
Therefore, the True Person acts without striving and does no
        harm,
    avoids grabbing and never loses hold.

People often ruin their ventures
    when they are on the verge of success.
So, be as careful at the end as at the beginning,
    and your work will not be ruined.

Therefore, the True Person seeks freedom from desire,
    does not value things that are hard to come by,
    learns without scholarship,
    brings people back to what they have passed by,
    and assists the ten thousand things to find their own
        natures;
    all without daring to interfere.

·65·

The ancients who practiced the Tao
    did not use it to enlighten the people,
    but rather to assist them in gaining simplicity.
The reason people are difficult to govern
    is because they are too clever.

Hence, a person who attempts
    to govern a country by cleverness
    will injure it.
Those who govern without cleverness
    will be a blessing to the land.
These are the two models.
Knowing these models is called the Mystic Virtue.
The Mystic Virtue is deep and so far-reaching
    that it can lead all things back
    toward great harmony.

·**66**·

How did the sea
    gain kingship of a hundred streams?
Because it takes the lower position.
Hence, it is king of a hundred streams.

Therefore, when True Persons are over the people
    they put themselves below the people by their speech.
When they lead the people
    they stand behind the people.

When True Persons are given places above the people
    they do not crush the people with their weight.
When they take their place ahead of the people
    they do not obstruct the people's progress.
That is why everything under heaven supports them gladly
    and does not tire of them.

Because they strive with no one,
    no one can ever strive with them.

·67·

Everyone under heaven says my Tao is great
    and resembles nothing else.
It is because it is great that it seems different.
If it were like anything on earth
    it would have been small from the beginning.

I have three treasures that I cherish and hold fast.
    The first is gentleness,
    the second is simplicity,
    the third is daring not to be first
        among all things under heaven.
Because of gentleness I am able to be courageous.
Because of simplicity I am able to be generous.
Because of daring not to be first
    I am able to lead.

If people forsake gentleness and attempt to be courageous,
    forsake simplicity and attempt to be generous,
    forsake the last place and attempt to get the first place,
    this is certain death.

Gentleness conquers in battle and protects in defense.
What heaven guards, it arms with the gift of gentleness.

·68·

A skilled warrior does not rush ahead of others.
A skilled fighter does not make a show of anger.
A skilled victor does not seek revenge.
A skilled employer does not act superior.

This is known as the virtue of not competing.
This is known as making use of the abilities of others.
This is known as being united with heaven
    as it was in ancient times.

·69·

The master soldiers have a saying:
>I dare not be the host but prefer to be the guest.
>I dare not advance an inch
>>but prefer to retreat a foot.

This is called marching without moving,
>rolling up a sleeve without baring an arm,
>capturing a foe without a battlefront,
>arming yourself without weapons.

There is no disaster greater than attacking
>and finding no enemy.
Doing so will cost you your treasure.
Thus it is that when opposing forces meet,
>victory will go to those
>who take no delight in the situation.

·**70**·

My words are easy to understand
    and easy to put into practice.
Yet no one under heaven understands them
    or puts them into practice.

My words have an ancestor. My actions are governed.

Because people do not understand this
    they do not understand me.
Those who understand me are few.
Those who follow me should be respected.

Therefore, the True Person wears homespun clothes
    and carries jade in the heart.

·71·

It is well to know that you do not know.
To think you know when you do not is sickness.

When you are sick of sickness you will no longer be sick.
True Persons are not sick because they are sick of sickness;
    this is the way to health.

·72·

When the people lack a sense of awe
    disaster will descend upon them.

Do not constrict their living space.
Do not harass them in their work.
If you do not oppress them, they will not weary of you.

Therefore, True Persons know themselves
    but make no show of themselves.
They know their value
    but do not exalt themselves.
They prefer this within to that without.

·73·

A person whose courage lies in daring will meet death.
A person whose courage lies in not daring
    will encounter life.
Of the two courses, either may be beneficial or harmful.

Heaven dislikes what it dislikes.
Who knows the reason why?
Even the True Person has difficulty with such a question.

The Tao of Heaven
    does not strive and yet it overcomes,
    does not speak and yet it gets responses,
    does not beckon and yet it attracts,
    is at ease and yet it follows a plan.

The net of heaven is cast wide.
Though the mesh is coarse, nothing ever slips through.

·74·

When the people do not fear death,
    of what use is it to threaten them with death?
If the people were always afraid of death
    and if those who did wrong
    would always be arrested and put to death,
    who would do wrong?

There is always a Lord of Execution
    whose duty it is to kill.
If you try to fill that function
    it is like trying to hew wood
    in place of a master carpenter.
You will probably injure your own hands.

·75·

Why are the people starving?
Because their leaders eat up too much of the tax-grain;
    that is why the people are starving.
Why are the people difficult to govern?
Because their leaders interfere;
    that is why the people are difficult to govern.
Why do the people treat death lightly?
Because their leaders are so grossly absorbed
    in the pursuit of living;
        that is why the people treat death lightly.

Indeed, it is wiser to ignore life altogether
    than to place too high a value on it.

·76·

At birth you are supple and soft.
At death you are stiff and hard.
Grass and trees are pliant and tender when living,
    but they are dry and brittle when dead.
Therefore, the stiff and hard are attendants of death,
    the supple and soft are attendants of life.

Thus, the hard weapon will be broken.
The mighty tree will invite the axe.

Therefore, the hard and mighty belong below;
    the yielding and gentle belong above.

·**77**·

The way of heaven is like the bending of a bow.
The high end is pulled down and the low end is raised up.
The excessive is diminished
    and the deficient is supplemented.

It is the way of heaven to take where there is too much
    in order to give where there is not enough.
The way of people is otherwise.
They take where there is not enough
    in order to increase where there is already too much.
Who will take from their own excesses
    and give to all under heaven?
Only those who hold to the Tao.

Therefore, the True Person benefits yet expects no reward,
    does the work and moves on.
There is no desire to be considered better than others.

·78·

Nothing under heaven is
softer or more yielding than water.
Yet it has no equal for attacking things
that are hard and stiff.
Nothing can withstand it.

Everyone knows that the yielding overcomes the stiff,
and the soft overcomes the hard.
Yet no one applies this knowledge.

Therefore, an Old One said:
Only a person who has accepted the country's dirt
is a leader worthy to offer sacrifice
at its shrines of earth and grain.
Only a person who takes up the country's burdens
deserves to be a leader
among those who dwell under heaven.

Straightforward words seem crooked.

·**79**·

Even though a truce is made between great enemies,
　　some enmity is bound to remain.
How can this be beneficial?

Therefore, the True Person
　　undertakes the obligations of the agreement
　　but makes no claim upon others.
The person who has Virtue shares with others.
The person who lacks Virtue takes from others.

The way of heaven has no favorites;
　　it always remains with what is good.

·80·

In a small country with few people:
>Though there are machines that would increase
>>production ten to a hundred times
>>they are not used.
>The people take death seriously and do not
>>travel about.

Though they have boats and carriages no one uses them.
Though they have armor and weapons,
>there is no occasion to display them.

The people give up writing
>and return to the knotting of cords.
They are satisfied with their food.
They are pleased with their clothes.
They are content with their homes.
They are happy in their simple ways.

Even though they live within sight of another country
>and can hear dogs barking and cocks crowing in it,
>still the people grow old and die
>without ever coming into conflict.

·81·

Sincere words are not elegant;
    elegant words are not sincere.
The good person does not argue;
    the person who argues is not good.
The wise do not have great learning;
    those with great learning are not wise.

True Persons do not hoard.
Using all they have for others, they still have more.
Giving all they have to others, they are richer than before.

The way of heaven is to benefit and not to harm.
The way of the True Person is to assist without striving
    in the unfolding of the story of the earth.

Here End
the Sayings of
The Old Ones